ASTROLOGY OF THE 12 ZODIAC SIGNS:

Personalities, Traits, Friendship, Compatibility, Love, Family And Career

About The Author

Claudius Adams has been practicing astrology for over 15 years, in the course of doing this, he has written for several publications around the world. Claudius presently runs a successful online astrology business where he brings astrology to reality with specific predictions, inspiration, and advice for present relevant things.

CONTENTS

WHAT YOU NEED TO KNOW ABOUT ASTROLOGY..1

THE ZODIAC SIGNS..4

    Air Signs:..4

    Water Signs: 5

    Fire Signs: 5

    Earth Signs:..5

QUALITIES OF ZODIAC SIGNS 7

ARIES ZODIAC SIGN..9

    Traits of Ariel-Born..12

    Other Traits of Aquarius-Born 13

TAURUS ZODIAC SIGN 16

    Traits of Taurus-Born 19

    Other Traits of Taurus-Born 20

GEMINI ZODIAC SIGN 23

Traits of Gemini-Born 25

Other Traits of Gemini-Born 26

CANCER ZODIAC SIGN 29

Traits of Cancer-Born 31

Other Traits of Cancer-Born 32

LEO ZODIAC SIGN 35

Traits of Leo-Born 37

Other Traits of Leo-Born 38

VIRGO ZODIAC SIGN 41

Traits of Virgo-Born 43

Other Traits of Virgo-Born 44

LIBRA ZODIAC SIGN 47

Traits of Libra-Born 49

Other Traits of Libra-Born 50

SCORPIO ZODIAC SIGN 53

    Traits of Scorpio-Born 55

    Other Traits of Scorpio-Born 56

SAGITTARIUS ZODIAC SIGN 58

    Traits of Sagittarius-Born 60

    Other Traits of Sagittarius-Born 61

CAPRICORN ZODIAC SIGN 63

    Traits of Capricorn-Born 65

    Other Traits of Capricorn-Born 66

AQUARIUS ZODIAC SIGN 69

    Traits of Aquarius-Born 72

    Other Traits of Aquarius-Born 73

PISCES ZODIAC SIGN 76

    Traits of Pisces-Born 78

    Other Traits of Pisces-Born 79

What You Need To Know About Astrology

Astrology can be considered to be both a science and an art. Astrology is called "art" because you need interpretation to bring the different aspects jointly together and work out an idea of the one's character traits.

Though, astrology is not considered a religion, it provides faith, comfort and a great understanding of where we live in, i.e. the world. Interpretations provide affirmations of one's future, but on important note, they are meant to direct us on ways to resolve issues and to enhance our relationships with our family, friends and partners. It's mainly a tool to discover our own deeper worlds in a different light and meet ourselves.

The goal of astrology is to help us to get better understanding of our positive characteristics and how to work on the negative ones. Astrology also helps us channel these energies on the positive traits.

Astrology counts on two key aspects - our birth potential and also the impacts of the stars & planets on our individual horoscope. This can aid you in choosing the right education and career path in order to live a good, prosperous and successful life. Your horoscope can be likened to a blueprint that got created exactly at the time you were born. That signifies that your birth chart is as unique as the fingerprints. A lot can be revealed about your personality and destiny from planet placement in your horoscope.

Astrology can help you find a compatible relationships and non-compatible ones. Horoscope compatibility assessment can improve your relationship with other zodiac symbols. Knowing your love potential can make you take necessary measures and explore opportunities that can lead to happy love and married life.

Astrology can also serve as a lifesaver, it makes you know the future problems and obstacles. You can save yourself from bearing any pain without doing much by believing and taking the precautions and advice suggested in the horoscope reading. Salvation doesn't come without doing much. This is the major problem with attitude to chart readings – everybody needs to put up a concerted effort to effect changes in their lives.

People have strong belief in astrology because curiosity is a fundamental human nature (the further one goes into astrology, the clearer things become) and that those before them did. We can make comparisons of zodiac signs with almost all areas of our lives, doing this will make one see that they are truly correct and insightful. Our horoscopes are very distinctive and they can aid us in finding and revealing natural qualities, strengths and weaknesses.

The Zodiac Signs

There are 12 known zodiac signs, and each sign possesses its own peculiarities such as: specific traits, strengths, weaknesses, desires and attitude on life and people. Astrologically analyzing the projection of the position of moon, the sun and the planets on the Ecliptic at the point of birth can give one a glimpse of a person's basic traits, flaws, preferences and fears.

Each of the 12 zodiac signs can be assigned into one of the following **four elements – Air, water, fire** and **Earth**. These elements denote an essential form of energy that works in each of us. These 4 elements help describe the unique personality types associated with astrological signs.

The 4 zodiac elements show profound influence on basic traits, character, behavior, emotions, thinking,

Air Signs: they are friendly, thinkers, intellectual, social, rational and analytical. They love communicating and relating with other people, social, gatherings, good books and philosophical discussions. They can be very superficial, but love giving advice. The Air Signs are: Aquarius, Libra and Gemini.

Water Signs: they are very sensitive, highly intuitive and exceptionally emotional, and they can be as mysterious as the ocean. Water signs love intimacy and heartfelt conversations. They do things openly in rare occasions and are always there to show support for their loved ones. The Water Signs are: Pisces, Cancer and Scorpio.

Fire Signs: they tend to be temperamental, passionate, adventurers with vast energy and dynamic. They get angry easily, but they can also forgive quickly. They are very strong physically, and can serve as inspiration for others. Fire signs are creative, self-aware, and idealistic people, always set to go into action. The Fire Signs are: Leo, Sagittarius and Aries.

Earth Signs: they are the signs that bring us down to the earth, i.e. they are "grounded". They are realistic, but can be very emotional. They have connections to our material reality and can also be turned to material goods. They are loyal, practical, mostly conservatives and stick by their people in hard times. The Earth Signs are: Capricorn, Virgo and Taurus.

Qualities of Zodiac Signs

The qualities of zodiac signs can be group into three, namely: Cardinal, Fixed and Mutable Qualities.

- **Cardinal Quality:** Cardinal quality signifies the energy of all new beginnings. Each of the zodiac sign of this quality possesses the ability and capability to make a sharp turn, change their own life or that of others. Looking around you, you'll observe that people born only under any of these Sun signs, wants, had or like to have the opportunity for a profound change of focus and direction in life.

  Zodiac signs of cardinal quality are Cancer, Aries, Capricorn and Libra. Each of them signifies a beginning of a season, and this makes them new, creative and innovative.

- **Fixed Quality:** immediately after something has started with a bang, fixed quality sign comes to calm and pacify the situation. Every season possesses a middle period, a point when it is clearly defined, and what to expect from it can be understood. This Fixed quality finds it difficult to make changes and people with the personal planet or sun in the sign of this quality will always be secretly set in their ways. Fixed signs are Aquarius, Leo, Taurus and Scorpio.

- **Mutable Quality:** Mutable quality refers to the quality of all the signs that have had enough already need to change. They all anticipate the new season, anything it may be, and they are already a mixture of the old and the new. It might be wrong to say that they signify the end of a thing, but rather a mixing of an end with a new beginning, intertwist. This represents the quality of the unexpected and constant changes that brings message about the future and what is yet to happen. All of the zodiac signs with this quality have the ability and capability to detect things before they come, and most of those gifted people that predict our future have these areas of the zodiac highlighted. Mutable signs are Pisces, Virgo, Gemini and Sagittarius.

Aries Zodiac Sign

Zodiac Element: Fire

Quality of Zodiac Sign: Cardinal Quality

Color: Red

Date: March 21 - April 19

Compatible Signs to Consider: Aquarius, Leo, Sagittarius, Gemini and Libra.

Aries is the 1st astrological zodiac sign, presence of Aries usually signifies the beginning of something dangerous and energetic. It starts with the first day of the spring when all things in nature wake up, while life starts to bloom. This sign signifies the beginning of one round or circle, the first zodiac sign, and the also leader in all aspects of the word. An Aries bravely leads the way from initial point zero, with a male forceful energy that makes clearance on the way at their front.

They continuously look for competition, speed and dynamics, being the top or first in everything - from social gatherings to work. Mars is the ruling planet for Aries, just like Leo and Sagittarius, and it belongs to the element of Fire. Aries relies on limitless energy, but when they hit the wall, they can't effect any breakage through (and after several trials), they'll make a cut and turn into a new direction.

Aries is one active zodiac sign. It is generally common in them, to take action, most times before they think deeply about it. Aries leads the top and rules with the head, often literally getting the direction of head first, moving forwards for focus and speed. Aries-born are naturally brave and they are rarely afraid of risk and trial. They have youthful energy, regardless of how they grow old, and quickly undertake any given tasks.

Aries-born are capable of completing several tasks at once, most times before lunch break due to the fact that the Sun in such high loftiness gives them an awesome organizational skills. Their weak points manifest when they get aggressive and show anger directed to other people or when they are impatient. Strong individuals born under Aries sign have a duty to fight for their targets, embracing teamwork and togetherness through this incarnation.

Traits of Ariel-Born

Aries loves: accepting leadership roles, wearing comfortable clothes, facing physical challenges, and partaking in individual sports.

Aries hates: work that does not need the use one's talents, time delay or being inactive.

Strengths: being honest, determined, courageous, enthusiastic, confident, optimistic, and passionate.

Weaknesses: they tend to be aggressive, impatient, short-tempered, moody and impulsive.

Other Traits of Aquarius-Born

- **Love and Sex:** An Aries is a very impassioned lover, most times even an addict to delight of the sexual encounters and flesh. Compatibility of Aries with other zodiac signs is very complex. Aries bonded in love may shower their partners with affection, to the extent that it can be in excess, forgetting to go through the feedback they get in return. When Aries develops strong feelings for love, they will make their feelings known to the individual they are in love with, without giving it a substantial thought.

   An Aries might be matched with themselves for the most cases, in deep respect for their own territories, but they are very compatible with some zodiac signs like - Aquarius, Leo, Sagittarius, Gemini and Libra.

- **Career and Money:** As a born leader, Aries will prefer to give orders rather than take them. Career and money is an aspect of life in where an Aries shines in brightest form. The environment where they work is the finest place for their creativity and ambition to flourish, with them striving to be better always. Their vast energy move and speed of mind always put them one step ahead of others. What they'll need to do to succeed is to adhere strictly to their chosen path and not relent on professional plans. In the face of challenges, an Aries quickly assesses the situation and bring forth a solution. They aren't bothered with competition, instead it encourages them to shine brighter. Aries-born can have great choice of careers in challenging environments and sports. They can enjoy their chosen career path as managers, soldiers, policemen, etc.

- **Friends and Family:** Aries-born easily get into communication, they are direct, truthful and honest in their attitude, and they will make a wonderful number of familiarities, acquaintances and connections in their lifetime. They are very tolerant and respectful of different individuals they come across, the openness they can display with simple presence. Their network of friends needs a varying number of strange personalities, this is to make them to feel like they have sufficient different opinions on personal issues they couldn't resolve. Though, they can cut off friendships with dishonesty or unclear intentions.

Aries-born are often conversant with where they want to go at a tender age. Even as young children, they can be difficult to control. In the absence or lack of patience and love from their parents, their intimate bonds could suffer later in life. Anger comes from the zodiac sign of Aries if there are too many limitations and restrictions on their way. Only when they are from tolerant families will they develop their bonds with a very easy flow.

Taurus Zodiac Sign

B

Zodiac Element: Earth

Quality of Zodiac Sign: Fixed Quality

Color: Pink, Green

Date: April 20 - May 20

Compatible Signs to Consider: Cancer, Capricorn, Virgo, Pisces

Taurus is the 2th astrological zodiac sign. Taurus represents an earth sign, just like Capricorn and Virgo, and possesses the ability and capability to view things from a practical, well-grounded and realistic way. Taurus is the zodiac sign that reaps the fruits of hard work. They feel the urgency to always be nurtured with love and beauty, physical pleasures, and love being turned to the material world. Taurus-Born are hedonistic, sensual and perceptible by touch, considering the fact that taste and touch are the most important of all the senses. They are conservative, stable, readily stick to their opinions until they get to the point of personal satisfaction.

Venus is the planet that rule Taurus, it is the planet of beauty, attraction, love, satisfaction, gratitude and creativity. This kind-hearted nature will make Taurus an excellent lover, artist, cook and gardener. They are faithful and hate criticism or sudden changes, somewhat dependent on individuals and emotions they seem not to be able to let go of. These personalities possesses the ability to lend a practical voice of reason in any disturbing and unhealthy situation, no matter what their emotions are.

They find it easy to stay on a project and make money for years, or till the work is completed. Their ability and capability to undertake and complete tasks is unearthly. Stubbornness in them can be taken as commitment. They are excellent employees, always being there for their loved ones, and are wonderful long-term friends or partners. Earthly qualities makes them conservative, materialistic or overprotective at times, with the world perspectives founded on their affection for money and wealth.

Traits of Taurus-Born

Taurus loves: cooking, gardening, romance, music, working with hands, putting on high quality clothes.

Taurus hates: wearing synthetic fabrics, sudden changes, insecurity of any form, complications.

Strengths: they are patient, reliable, devoted, practical, responsible and stable

Weaknesses: they tend to be uncompromising, stubborn and possessive.

Other Traits of Taurus-Born

- **Love and Sex:** Patience is highly needed when having love affairs with Taurus-born. All pleasurable senses such as touch and smell, are of utmost importance to Taurus-born, they are sensual but they also need enough time to relax in their sexual adventures and create a safe environment. They become a bit over-emotional, when they make enough intimacy with their partner, most times even needy, and their emotions have to be kept in check, embracing change and ideas of their loved one while holding on to practical reasoning at all times. Relationships on long-term with them often involve choosing partners from the particular social environment that can be able to meet their intellectual needs and expectations of their close friends and family.
- **Career and Money:** Taurus-born usually love money and can work assiduously to earn it. As an employee or somebody in a position of power, their strengths lies in them being reliable,

patient, hardworking and thorough. The basis to understanding their working routine is stability. Their quest for material rewards and pleasures is the motif behind building their own sense of value and also achieving a luxurious, yet practical way to life. Their role is observed as a step to make it feasible.

Taurus-born are well organized when it comes to their finances. They take responsibility, save funds for rainy day, and also keep pension.

Occupations that best fit Taurus-born include: agriculture, art, banking, and culinary skills.

- **Friends and Family:** Taurus-born are very loyal and always willing to stretch out a hand of friendship and companionship, though, until they build trust for all new social contacts they make, they can also be closed up to the outside world. Their friendships starts in childhood stage with a high tendency to elapse till lifetime. When they make a defined intimate relationship to another partner, they will do anything to make the relationship works even in the hard times.

At home, family matters is of utmost importance to all Taurus. They love kids, respect family routine, and cherish time spent with individuals who love them.

Gemini Zodiac Sign

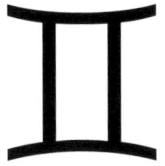

Zodiac Element: Air

Quality of Zodiac Sign: Mutable Quality

Color: Yellow, Light-Green

Date: May 21 - June 20

Compatible Signs to Consider: Aries, Aquarius, Leo, Libra, Sagittarius

Gemini is the 3rd astrological zodiac sign. Gemini belongs to the air signs, along with Aquarius and Libra, and this creates a nexus between it and all aspects of our mind. They are perceptive, smart and expressive. Mercury is the planet that rules Gemini sign, Mercury represents writing, communication and movement. Gemini-born often have feelings that their second half is nowhere to be found, so they are eternally seeking new friends, colleagues, mentors and people to speak to.

Gemini shows two different people in one and you'll unsure which one you will turn to. They love to have fun, very communicative and sociable, with a tendency to be thoughtful and restless, and suddenly get serious. They are attracted to the world itself, very curious, with a constant notion that there is limited time to experience anything they like to see.

Their open and changeable minds makes them excel well as writers, journalists and artist, and their flexible skills do well in driving, trading, team sports. The sign is a fun loving, versatile and very inquisitive, being thoughtful to experience everything in the world. This traits actually makes their character never boring and also inspiring.

Traits of Gemini-Born

Gemini loves: reading books or magazines, listening to music, going on short trips around the town, chatting with nearly anyone.

Gemini hates: Being confined, being alone, and repetition.

Strengths: they are affectionate, curious, gentle, and adaptable, they have ability to learn quickly and also exchange ideas.

Weaknesses: they tend to be inconsistent, nervous and indecisive.

Other Traits of Gemini-Born

- **Love and Sex:** Gemini-born spots love first through verbal contact or communication, and take this as important as having physical contact with their lover. Gemini could spend ample of their time with different partners, this can go on till they are able to get the right one which could match their energy and intellect. When they eventually get their match, they are very faithful and determined to always value their heart.

  The highest problem in the love life of Gemini is not having an emotion that lasts long, especially as they grow older and reality dawns that they have been in a disappointing bonds. Gemini can make a sharp turn, leaving their lovers behind, but in some cases, some partners could follow in their pace, in getting ready to build a strong loving foundation that can stand a test of time.

- **Career and Money:** They are inventive, innovators, skillful and very smart. They can multitask, solve problems, bring new ideas to life, and can thrive well in a dynamic working environment. A career that gives them the freedom to freely communicate while being kept on the move and busy most times, is an excellent fit for them. Deciding between pleasure and practicality can be a hard choice for Gemini. The best careers that are best of fit for them are: trading, law, inventions, writings, oratory and preaching.

  A strong grounding is needed to keep their finances organized and checked, granting them a sense of security and confidence they aren't even aware they need.

- **Friends and Family:** Gemini-born love spending their time with friends and families, and are very social. They have abundant of social contacts, and loves chatting, searching for understanding. They always look for strong willed individuals to communicate with.

Family is also very important to a Gemini-born, especially when they build a great emotional bonds with their children. Instability they show towards their partners don't reflect on their family as such, and they tend to have a calmer and more modest approach to people they share a home with.

Cancer Zodiac Sign

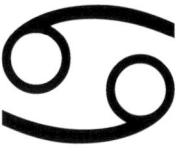

Zodiac Element: Water

Quality of Zodiac Sign: Cardinal Quality

Color: White

Date: June 21 - July 22

Compatible Signs to Consider: Capricorn, Virgo, Taurus, Virgo, Pisces and Scorpio.

Cancer is the 4th astrological zodiac sign. Cancer belongs to the water signs, just like Scorpio and Pisces. They are ruled by the moon, various phases of lunar cycle intensify the internal mysteries attributed to them, and also create emotional patterns often beyond their control. Cancer-born are guided by their emotions and heart, they can have a difficult time while trying to blend into the world that revolves around them.

Cancers are deeply sentimental and intuitive, they can be one most challenging of all the zodiac. They are very sensitive, emotional and care well about family and home issues, very sympathetic and are well attached to personalities they keep close. Cancer-born are very loyal and able show empathy with other people's sufferings.

Impatience, selfishness, manipulation, self-pity or even lack of love will show through attitudinal and mood changes later in life. They are always ready to offer assistance to others, just as the same way they try to avoid conflict and disagreement. They rarely profit from combat of any type, always choosing to fight someone bigger, stronger and more powerful than they could imagined.

As children, they lack adequate defensive and coping technique for the outer world, and have to be nurtured with enough care and understanding, since that is what they'll give in return.

Traits of Cancer-Born

Cancer loves: home-based hobbies, helping their loved ones, relaxing near water, having a good meal with friends.

Cancer hates: seeing strangers, being criticized by mom, revealing their personal life.

Strengths: they are highly imaginative, tenacious, loyal, sympathetic, persuasive and emotional.

Weaknesses: they are pessimistic, insecure, moody, suspicious and manipulative.

Other Traits of Cancer-Born

- **Love and Sex:** Cancer is a dedicated and emotional sign. Cancer-born are caring and gentle, they display their sensibility to the world without having thought of being hurt. Cancers always choose a partners who can understand them through silent contact or non-verbal form of communication, and also share daily routine. Their love may not last long with superficial or unreliable partners. They are ready to make some unhealthy compromises, just to keep their image of a family moving, and could choose selfish or abusive partners. Having a life together with their lovers and shared responsibility can make them feel safe, secure and get ready for the next stages in life.

  Deep understanding and compassion that a Cancer chose to show you should never be taken for granted, else they will show you the other side of the coin.

- **Career and Money:** If Cancers are left alone to perform a task, they usually do better compared with when they are surrounded with other people. They are always focused on the task and very loyal to their employer.

Money and security are also very important, this is the main reason to work as much as they do. They easily get money and are not used to expending it all in a day. It is their aim to invest and save.

They will have excellent careers in: nursing, gardening, housekeeping, decorations and politics.

- **Friends and Family:** Cancer-born will gladly be ready to meet and connect with friends and new social contacts, but they can be very sensitive to personalities not approved by their immediate surrounding. They have high respect for people they communicate to freely, they view all contacts through their emotional point rather than status.

Cancer is a family sign. Cancer-born diligently preserve memories of family, they are deeply sentimental and care more about their home or family bonds more than other zodiac signs.

Leo Zodiac Sign

♌

Zodiac Element: Fire

Quality of Zodiac Sign: Fixed Quality

Color: Orange, Yellow

Date: July 23 - August 22

Compatible Signs to Consider: Gemini, Aries, Libra, Sagittarius.

Leo is the 5th astrological zodiac sign. Leo belongs to the fire signs, just like Aries and also Sagittarius. The fire elements make them kindhearted and be in love with life. They have ability to use their mind to provide solutions to most difficult problems. The Sun rules Leo sign. Litcrally as well as metaphorically, this zodiac sign worships this fiery structure (Sun) in the sky. They search for constant growth of ego and self-awareness. Their personality can make them desire for anything they need, but could just as easily unwittingly ignore the needs of others in their quest for personal gain and status. When Leo-born become too attached to their gains, they become an easy target by other people who see them, and ready to be taken down.

Leo-born are born leaders. They are creative, self-confident, dramatic, dominant and extremely hard to resist, and are able to achieve everything they aspire to in any aspect of life they focus on. Leo, which has a natural inclination to rule has a status of "king of the jungle". Leo's generosity and loyalty often attract friends to them, they are attractive and self-confident. Leo has ability to unite different groups of individuals and lead them as one towards a shared goal. Collaboration with other people is even made easier with their healthy sense of humor.

Traits of Leo-Born

Leo loves: taking holidays, being admired, going to theatre, expensive things, having fun with friends, and bright colors.

Leo hates: facing difficult reality, being ignored, and not being respected like a king or queen

Strengths: being passionate, generous, creative, warm-hearted, humorous and cheerful.

Weaknesses: they tend to be stubborn, self-centered, arrogant, lazy and rigid.

Other Traits of Leo-Born

- **Love and Sex:** when Leos fall in love, they are loyal, fun, respectful and very generous towards their partners. They will assume the leadership role in any relationship, and they rely strongly on their quest for initiative and independency. This may be tiring to their lover most times, especially if they become too overbearing imposing their will on the partner. Leo needs a partner that is on the same intellectual level as them, reasonable and self-aware.

  Leo's sex life is an adventure, full of fun and very energetic. They have clear understanding and insight on boundaries between love and sex, but might fail to see the importance of emotional connection and intimacy to the quality of their sex life.

- **Career and Money:** They are energetic, ambitious, optimistic and creative. Their dedication to work can make them do everything just right. They find themselves in best possible situation when they are their own bosses or manage people with minimum control from their bosses as possible. Anything that will put them in a leadership position will naturally spur them into action.

They love to be surrounded by new or trendy things, though make money easily, spending it less responsibly when compared with some other zodiac signs. They could provide financial help to many friends, lending support to them in harsh times.

Some jobs that best fit Leo-born include: acting and entertainment, management, politics and education.

- **Friends and Family:** Leo rarely stay alone, they are faithful, generous and a truly loyal friend. They are born with a certain commitment to people's values and to help others, they do so even if it costs a lot time and energy. They are reliable and very strong, Leo possesses the ability to appeal to almost everybody and has the capability to host different events and celebrations with people that can bring out the best in them.

Leo-born do not think about family matters first when they lie to bed at night or wake up in the morning. They tend to be independent as early as possible. Besides, Leo-born can do anything to shield and protect their loved ones. They are proud of their ancestral roots at all times.

Virgo Zodiac Sign

♍

Zodiac Element: Earth

Quality of Zodiac Sign: Mutable Quality

Color: Grey, Pale-Yellow

Date: August 23 – September 22

Compatible Signs to Consider: Taurus, Cancer, Pisces, Scorpio, Capricorn

Virgo is the 6th astrological zodiac sign. It is an Earth sign that fits perfectly between Taurus & Capricorn. This will bring out strong character, in one that prefers to be well-organized, conservative and has a lot of practicality in their undertaken. Virgo-born have an organized life, their dreams and goals still have strictly guided borders in their mind, even when they relinquish a chaos. They're constantly bordered about missing a detail that will be difficult to fix, they can get flounder in details, becoming overly concerned and critical about issues that care less about.

Mercury is the planet that rules this zodiac sign. Virgos possess a well-developed and also high sense of speech and writing, along with other means of communication.

Virgo-born always pay attention to the details, no matter how little it is, and also their high sense of humanity will make them one of the most careful zodiac signs. Their approach to life is methodical, this is to ensure that anything is not left to chance. Their heart can be closed for the outer world, due to their tenderness, this sign often misunderstood, because they won't agree that their feelings are genuine, relevant or true when opposed to reason. Also, the symbolism behind the name typically represents nature, born with a feeling that they are experiencing all things for the afresh.

Traits of Virgo-Born

Virgo loves: healthy foods, animals, reading books, nature and cleanliness.

Virgo hates: asking for help, rudeness, taking center stage.

Strengths: they are analytical, loyal, kind, practical and hardworking.

Weaknesses: they tend to show shyness, overly critical of self and others, worry, all work and no play.

Other Traits of Virgo-Born

- **Love and Sex:** Virgos rarely have direct assertion for love, but the beauty in their emotional self-expression can be brought out by intimacy. They will prefer a stable relationship to having just fun or temporary lovers, with exception of if they become one. They use their perfunctory communication to win hearts.

Virgos are intellectually and methodically dominant, they tend to have in their mind an equation that their partner has to follow.

Virgo sign is easily likened to the symbolism of a virgin, but have mutable quality. Their quest for change often overrides their moral boundaries or self-imposed limitations when it comes to sex.

Trust with a Virgo should be built patiently slowly and steadily. Also their partner has a chance to be cared for, only if they give sufficient to warrant special treatment by Virgo.

- **Career and Money:** Virgos methodology makes them excel at jobs that need problem solving, good organization, working with their minds and hands, and dealing with paperwork. Perfection should be expected from their work, as other signs do not have an eye for details like Virgo. They are hard-working, practical and analytical, and always know the exact point to look for the cause of any problem.

  Virgo sign represents every practical and used things, it is in the nature of these personalities to save funds. They view irrational spending as a very bad habit of being spoiled, they also show preference for practical solutions that won't cost much.

  They serve humankind best if they decide to become nurses, doctors or psychologists.

- **Friends and Family:** having an intimate friendship with any Virgo-born will always earned good deeds. Virgos always know how to solve a problem, they are excellent advisors.

This can make them extremely useful and helpful to have around.

Virgos show high dedication to their family and are very attentive to sick and elderly individuals. They have deep understanding of tradition and also the significance of responsibility. Virgos are proud of everything that makes their mind be as dominant, and also their upbringing.

Libra Zodiac Sign

♎

Zodiac Element: Air

Quality of Zodiac Sign: Cardinal Quality

Color: Pink, Green

Date: September 23 - October 22

Compatible Signs to Consider: Sagittarius, Aquarius, Gemini, Leo.

Libra is the 7th astrological zodiac sign. Libra is an Air sign, that fits perfectly between Gemini & Aquarius, this gives Libra-born a strong intellect and constant mental response to stimuli. They derive inspirations from having insurmountable discussions and reading good books. Libra-born have to be careful when having conversation with other people, for when they are coerced to take decision about something coming their way and choose sides, they instantly realize that they might be surrounded by wrong personalities or be in the wrong place.

Venus planet rules the Libra sign, this makes Libra-born great lovers and also fond of costly material things. Their lives need enrichment by art, music and beautiful spots they have opportunity to visit.

Libras are fair, peaceful and they hate staying alone. Partnership is very significant for them, to serve as their mirror and somebody giving them the room to be the mirror by themselves. These personalities are attracted by symmetry balance, they are in a frequent chase for equality and justice. They are ready to do almost everything to avoid conflict, sticking to peace whenever possible

Traits of Libra-Born

Libra loves: peace and harmony, the outdoors, gentleness, and sharing with others.

Libra hates: injustice, violence, conformity and loudmouths.

Strengths: they are diplomatic, gracious, cooperative, social and fair-minded.

Weaknesses: they are indecisive, carry grudge, self-pity and avoids confrontations.

Other Traits of Libra-Born

- **Love and Sex:** the top priority in a Libra's life is finding a compatible partners. When they go into a romantic relationship with someone, maintaining and sustaining peace and harmony become their primary goal and the most significant thing. Their unending dedication to every relationship makes their compatibility with others encouraging.

Libra represents a sign of marriage, this makes Libra-born open for traditional walkways of love. In some ways, every Libra looks for a partner who has the zeal to set defined boundaries, like he is expecting to get protection from them, without their dignity being endangered in the process.

Libras look out for deep, healthy and meaningful relationship, though they don't have issue when relating with individuals they aren't close to. The only real gratification in their love life will come from complete surrender of soul and body.

When Libras make up their mind to be with someone, they have already made a good choice, but it will help in knowing any obstacles on their way to achieving happiness.

- **Career and Money:** Libras won't show commitment to work without setting aside sufficient time for their private life or loved ones. They can also be affectionate leaders, though, occasionally they don't have the initiative needed in organizing people who work for them, and will work diligently to deserve any entitlement that comes their way.

In term of finances, they strike balance between saving and spending excellently well, though they have penchant for fine clothes and fashion, they rarely let their wish for spending get their best.

In their quest for truth or justice, they are good lawyers & judges. They can also be successful as composers, diplomats, and designers.

- **Friend and Family:** Libra-born are highly social and always put their friends in the public attention, but sometimes raise the bar of their expectation too high. They select friendships that give them superiority over the person standing in their front.

In the family, they can often share guilt among family members by even being unaware of doing so. In continuous quest for harmony, these personalities have a propensity to agree with their siblings and parents just to avoid conflict or disagreement, being the one to retreat when a problem comes their way.

Scorpio Zodiac Sign

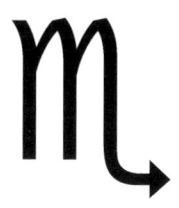

♏

Zodiac Element: Water

Quality of Zodiac Sign: Fixed Quality

Color: Scarlet, Red

Date: October 23 - November 21

Compatible Signs to Consider: Cancer, Pisces, Virgo, Capricorn.

Scorpio is the 8th astrological zodiac sign. It is a Water sign. A Scorpio-born lives to experience and show emotions. Though emotions are very significant for Scorpio, they show them differently when compared with other water signs. They are good at keeping secrets and are good leaders because they show dedication in what they do.

Scorpio-born are determined, decisive, passionate and assertive personalities, and will do a thorough research until they get truth. Scorpio is always aware of the happenings and also features remarkably in resourcefulness.

Pluto, a planet of regeneration and transformation, rules Scorpio zodiac sign. Scorpio-born are known by their cool and calm conduct, and also by their strange appearance. Some assume that Scorpio-born are fierce, this might be because they have deep understanding of the rules governing the universe. Scorpios dislikes dishonesty, they can be very suspicious and jealous, and so they need to learn means of adaptation to different human behavioral conducts. Their braveness make them have many friends.

Traits of Scorpio-Born

Scorpio loves: being right, truth, facts, teasing, longtime friends, and a grand passion.

Scorpio hates: passive people, revealing secrets, dishonesty.

Strengths: they are brave, resourceful, stubborn, passionate, and a true friend

Weaknesses: they tend to be jealous, violent and secretive.

Other Traits of Scorpio-Born

- **Love and Sex:** Scorpio-born are very passionate. Scorpio being the most sensual zodiac sign, intimacy is of utmost importance to them. They want an honest and intelligent people as partners. Scorpios are very dedicated and faithful when they fall in love. However, they carefully enter into any relationship, because most times they need enough of time to build respect or trust for partners.
- **Career and Money:** anytime a Scorpio sets a goal, they don't give up. Scorpios are fantastic in solving skills, thorough approach, management and creating.

  Their zeal to focus on with enough determination makes them very suitable as managers. They do not mix business with other things like friendship.

  Scorpio-born are well disciplined to stick to the budget plan, but they also don't have fear for hard work to bring themselves into a stable financial disposition. However, they are not likely to spend much. Scorpios show respects to other people, so they expect the same in return. People under this powerful zodiac sign function at their best level when they work as: physician, researcher, scientist, sailor, cop, detective, psychologist and business manager.

- **Friends and Family:** the two attributes that make Scorpio a great friend are honesty and fairness. Scorpio-born are very loyal and dedicated, when it comes to working. They are very intelligent, full of surprises, and quick-witted, so they would feel better to be in the midst of fun loving people. They'll give you anything you need, provided you do not let them down – and if otherwise, there's no return. Scorpio-born show emotions, when they are in pain, it is not possible to make them feel better. They are dedicated and they take proper care of their family.

Sagittarius Zodiac Sign

Zodiac Element: Fire

Quality of Zodiac Sign: Mutable Quality

Color: Blue

Date: November 22 - December 21

Compatible Signs to Consider: Aries, Leo, Aquarius, Libra.

Sagittarius is the 9th astrological zodiac sign. It is a fire sign and one of the greatest travelers among all zodiac signs. Sagittarius needs to be frequently in touch with the world so as to have much experience as possible. Jupiter (the largest planet of the zodiac) is the planet that rules Sagittarius sign. Their enthusiasm is limitless, and therefore Sagittarius-born are energetic, possesses an intense curiosity and a great sense of humor. Their philosophical view and open mind motivates them to travel around the world searching for the meaning of life.

Sagittarius are enthusiastic, optimistic and extrovert, and love changes. They are able to change their ideas into concrete actions, they can also go any length to achieve their goals.

Their greatest treasure is freedom, because only then they can travel freely and explore several philosophies and cultures. Their honesty often make them tactless and impatient when they need to do or say something, therefore, it is significant to learn to express themselves in a socially acceptable and more tolerant way.

Traits of Sagittarius-Born

Sagittarius loves: travelling, freedom, philosophy, and being outdoors.

Sagittarius hates: being constrained, clingy persons, off-the-wall theories, and details.

Strengths: they are idealistic, generous and have great sense of humor.

Weaknesses: they tend to be impatient, will say anything no matter how undiplomatic, and promise more than can deliver.

Other Traits of Sagittarius-Born

- **Love and Sex:** Sagittarius-born are humorous and very playful, this shows that they will derive unlimited pleasure from having fun with their partners. Open partners will certainly suit an expressive and passionate Sagittarius who is ready to try almost everything.

  Sagittarius sign has a thin line in between love and sex. Different problems in their bedroom due to their love for change and diversity. But when they are genuinely in love, they are very faithful, dedicated and loyal. They want their partners to be sensitive, intellectual and expressive.

- **Career and Money:** Sagittarius-born will do everything they can to achieve any thought that comes to their minds. They always have what to say in any given circumstances. They are great salespeople.

  Sagittarius as a fun lover enjoys making and spending money. They are considered to be the happiest zodiac sign. They can take risks and are very optimistic.

Sagittarius favors several tasks and dynamic atmosphere. They function at their best levels when they work as: photographer, a travel agent, artist, researcher, ambassador, importer and exporter.

- **Friends and Family:** Sagittarius-born are very generous, fun-filled and always surrounded by friends and loved ones. They love laughing and enjoying the variation of culture and life, so they will easily get attracted to many friends around them. They are dedicated to do almost anything when it comes to family matter.

Capricorn Zodiac Sign

♑

Zodiac Element: Earth

Quality of Zodiac Sign: Cardinal Quality

Color: Brown, Black

Date: December 22 - January 19

Compatible Signs to Consider: Taurus, Scorpio, Virgo, Pisces.

Capricorn is the 10th astrological zodiac sign. It is an earth sign, just like Taurus & Virgo, and the last sign in the trio of grounding and practicality. They don't only focus on the material world, but also they possess the ability to utilize most out of it. Capricorns have a hard time to accept the differences of others that are too distinctive from their character, and out of despair might try to foist their traditional values aggressively.

Saturn (a planet which represents restrictions of all kinds) is the planet that rules Capricorn. Its influence on Capricorns makes them practical, responsible, distant and unforgiving, cold, and susceptible to the feeling of guilt and turning to the past. To make their own life more positive and lighter, they need to learn to forgive.

Capricorn sign signifies time and responsibility. Capricorn-born are traditional and usually very serious by nature. They possess an inner state of freedom that enables important trajectory in their personal and professional lives. They have the capability to lead the way, make realistic and solid plans, or manage several people who work for them at any specific time, they are masters of self-control. They can learn from their errors and get to the top based singularly on their expertise and experience.

Traits of Capricorn-Born

Capricorn loves: music, understated status, family, tradition, and quality craftsmanship.

Capricorn hates: almost everything at some particular points.

Strengths: they are disciplined, responsible, have self-control, and are good managers

Weaknesses: they tend to be unforgiving, condescending, know-it-all, expecting the worst.

Other Traits of Capricorn-Born

- **Love and Sex:** Their relationships with other zodiac signs can be a bit challenging owing to their tedious character, but any feeling shared as a result of deep emotional place, will serve as reward for their partner's energy. Shown sensitivity emanates from acts rather than words, enough time is often needed for them to open up to chat about their real emotional problems. It is somehow difficult to win over the heart and attention of Capricorns, but anytime their heart melts, they show commitment for a lifetime.

  Capricorns may not show emotion or compassion when relating with their loved ones. They will give with full devotion to a normal life, and their partner will have ease to rely on them, or use them as a yardstick for any personal endeavor. Still, Capricorn isn't somebody ready to compromise much, and tends to have the urgency to create a difficulty only to resolve it or feel somehow sad that it was never resolved at all.

- **Career and Money:** Capricorns value hard work and loyalty over anything, and keep personalities with these characters close even when they are intellectually inferior. Their honesty, perseverance and dedication make them achieve their goals. Capricorn gets the job done, without minding long hour duration, and show commitments to the final results.

  Capricorns truly value money in their lives, and they won't have much problem in saving funds for a rainy day, as long as their debts do not consume their actual capabilities.

  Occupations that best fit Capricorns include: finance, calculations, management and programming.

- **Friends and Family:** Capricorns are open-hearted, warm, intelligent, honest, reliable and stable, and this makes Capricorn-born extremely good friends and loyal. They don't take much friends, but get more fascinated to people.

They have deep understanding of family traditions. Capricorns have connection to things from their past and childhood days, and they like to bring out these memories anytime a holiday or birthday approaches.

Aquarius Zodiac Sign

Zodiac Element: Air

Quality of Zodiac Sign: Fixed Quality

Color: Silvery or Light-Blue

Date: January 20 - February 18

Compatible Signs to Consider: Libra, Aries, Sagittarius or Gemini

Aquarius is the 11th astrological zodiac sign. Aquarius uses his mind at every point of opportunity, it is an air sign. They always feel bored and lack inspiration to get best result in the absence of mental stimulation.

Uranus is the ruling planet of Aquarius, Uranus possesses a shy, sometimes aggressive or abrupt nature and also gives a visionary quality to Aquarius, the power of easy and quick transformation, and they are called thinkers, humanists and progressives. They feel better in a group of people, because of this, they constantly try to be surrounded by other individuals.

Aquarius-born have ability to perceive the future, they know exactly what they like to do in five or ten years to come.

Aquarius-born are very quiet and timid, but they can be energetic and eccentric. They are highly intellectual individuals and deep thinkers who love rendering help to others. They can be able to see without preconception, on the two sides, this makes them solution providers to problems.

Though they can easily get used to the energy around them, Aquarius-born have a great need to be alone some times and stay away from many things, in order to regain power. Individuals born under this Aquarius sign, view world as a place where possibilities abound.

One of the biggest challenges for Aquarius-born, is having the feeling that they are constrained or limited.

Due to their quest for equality and freedom for all, they always try to maintain movement and freedom of speech. Aquarius-born are said to be insensitive persons and cold in characters, their mechanism of defending themselves against premature intimacy. They need to learn to show their emotions in a healthy way, and also need to trust others.

Traits of Aquarius-Born

Aquarius loves: a good listener, having intellectual conversation, having fun with friends and loved ones, helping other individuals, fighting for a cause.

Aquarius hates: being alone and boring situations, getting broken promises and limitations, people disagreeing with them.

Top Strengths: they are original, humanitarian, progressive and independent.

Top Weaknesses: they are temperamental, they shy away from emotional expression, uncompromising, and staying aloof.

Other Traits of Aquarius-Born

- **Love and Sex:** only an interesting conversation with an individual can attract Aquarius. The characteristics that fit well in the view of life of this Aquarius zodiac sign include: good communication, being imaginative, open and willing to risk. The compatibility of this Aquarius to other signs can be complex and look complicated. Anybody who wants to go into a long-term relationship affair with this dynamic person (Aquarius) needs to have honesty, sincerity and integrity. When in love, they show commitment, loyalty not at all possessive – in term of giving freedom to their lovers which will make them consider them as equals.
- **Career and Money:** Aquarius is known to be a visionary and focused sign who loves to engage in activities for the betterment of humanity. Their high level of intellect joined with their readiness to share their ideas and talents can

give inspiration for many who work or lives in their immediate environment.

When it comes to business and money, Aquarius has ability to strike a balance between saving and spending money. Aquarius are well soothed to their preferred feel for a style and they are not shy to show it.

Suitable careers for this sign include: writing, acting, photography, piloting or teaching. The most suitable environment for them is one which gives no limitations to solving the problem with no strict guidelines. Aquarius, if given the chance to express their unconventional talent, can gain tremendous success.

- **Friends and Family:** though Aquarius are communicative, they still need enough time to move close to people, being close to them might mean vulnerability, this is because of their highly sensitive nature.. Aquarius can do anything for a friend or his loved one to the extent of self-sacrifice if need be. A friend to

Aquarius should possess the qualities: integrity, creativity and intellect. The expectations are nothing less when it comes to family. Though they tend to have a sense of duty to their relatives, they won't entertain close ties if the different expectations in friendship are not met.

Pisces Zodiac Sign

♓

Zodiac Element: Water

Quality of Zodiac Sign: Mutable Quality

Color: Purple, Violet, Lilac, Sea green

Date: February 19 - March 20

Compatible Signs to Consider: Taurus, Scorpio, Cancer, Capricorn.

Pisces is the 12th astrological zodiac sign. Pisces is a Water sign of mutable modality and speaks of the difference in our waters. It begins at the end of winter and get us prepared for the starting of spring. This sign might represent the zodiac sign of ends, but it can be also a place of transformation from darkness to light and from death to life. It is the pleasing expectation of spring.

Neptune is the ruling planet for Pisces, therefore, Pisces possesses an artistic talent that are more instinctive than others. Neptune is well connected to music, so Pisces show music inclination in the earliest phases of life. They are compassionate, generous and extremely caring & faithful. Individuals born under the Pisces sign possess an instinctive knowledge of the life cycle, hence can achieve a better emotional relationship with others.

Pisces-born are very friendly, this trait makes them keep company of very different personalities. They are selfless and are always ready to help others, without expecting any return.

Pisces as a Water sign is characterized by compassion and express emotional capability. Pisces-born are well reputed by their knowledge, this might be different under another planet – Uranus, where Pisces can as martyr, just to get attention. Pisces are always forgiving and never judgmental, they are known to be most tolerant sign among the zodiac signs.

Traits of Pisces-Born

Pisces loves: staying alone, listening to music, romance, sleeping, swimming, spiritual themes, and visual media.

Pisces hates: being criticized, know-it-all personalities, cruelty of any form, the past coming back to haunt.

Strengths: they are compassionate, gentle, wise, artistic, intuitive, and musical.

Weaknesses: being sad, desire to escape reality, being fearful, overly trusting, can be a martyr.

Other Traits of Pisces-Born

- **Love and Sex:** Pisces-born are very romantic in nature. They are gentle, loyal, passionate lovers and explicitly generous and liberal to their partners. Pisces have a need to feel a real impact of connecting with their partners. Short-term relationships are not peculiar to this Pisces sign. They are very caring and blindly loyal in love and their relationships.
- **Career and Money:** Pisces fit best in a position that their creative skills will come to the forward. They're intuitive and frequently dreamy.

    The zodiac sign is very hard-working, compassionate, reliable and dedicated. They can be great problem solvers. On most part, Pisces-born don't think about money much, instead, they are always more focused on their goals and dreams, but enough money has to be made to put their dreams into reality. In this aspect, there are possibilities of two sides of the Pisces - on first hand, they can spend a lot of money without much thought, also on the other hand they can be quite stingy. They function at their best level when they work as a/an: architect, attorney, musician, game designer, veterinarian and social worker.

- **Friends and Families:** Pisces-born can be ones best friends that may exist, they are caring, loyal, compassionate, devoted and very gentle. In some cases, they can put their friend's needs in front of theirs. When problem arises among friends or in the family, they put in their best to resolve it amicably. Pisces can notice if something goes wrong, even before it takes place at all, they don't hesitate to express their how they feel and their perception to other people around them. They also expect other people to be very open to them as well. Effective communication with friends, loved ones and family is very important to them.

Printed in Great Britain
by Amazon